The Beginner's Guide to Medical Marijuana Stock Profits: The top 10 of 2018 & Many Other Promising Marijuana Stocks

Dedication

This book is dedicated to Tim Heitz who taught me a great deal about pot stocks. He helped me more than quadruple my initial investment and told me a lot about many pot companies and why they were solid investments as well as helping me with the final editing of this book. Thanks, Tim!

Reader: If you like this book, PLEASE go to the kindle page from which you ordered it and LEAVE FEEDBACK... it needn't be long or take more than one minute and it will mean a great deal to me. Thanks!

Contents

Introduction

(Why buy Pot Stocks & Why NOW)
So, you would like to cash in on the greatest opportunity since Xerox, Apple and Microsoft stock became available to the public? Here is everything you need to get started NOW, even if you only have $100 to start with. This book will describe in detail the top ten pot stock earners of 2018 as well as many others well worth considering.

I started with $1,000.00 and about ten months later my account was worth about $4,500 – strictly on the gains earned by the stocks I purchased. Information is key and this book has a lot of information in a very small space so that you can, without spending hundreds of hours, make educated investments with a high likelihood of massive earnings.

As of this writing forty-seven of the fifty states have already passed some form of legal use of marijuana. Equally exciting is that the Federal Government just passed legislation making it legal to grow "hemp." (Hemp is the term to legally describe the cannabis plant if it has no more than 0.03% THC - the cannabinol that produces mind altering experience found in cannabis known as "marijuana"). Hemp is what is most often used to extract CBD – the cannabinol most used for medical purposes – and the Federal Government has now sanctioned PERSCRIPTION use of CBDs.

The bottom line is that the US is not moving toward Federal legalization, it is racing toward federal legalization. In addition, in Canada all forms of cannabis (recreational and medical) is now legal and Canadian firms have stock available for purchase on the US stock exchange. Yes, US companies are also available but are currently handicapped by US sanctions preventing them from access to banking – deposits, loans, etc. When this becomes available to them in coming months, their businesses are set to expand exponentially.

NOW is the time to get into these stocks.... But which ones? Small companies can go bust...but they can also make stock holders a fortune. Remember Xerox, Apple and Microsoft. Imagine buying them the first year... and that is the situation we are in today in the marijuana industry. However, which stocks from over 650 marijuana based companies have the best chance of making it to the really big time... this book will tell you what my personal experience has led me to believe are the important factors to consider and which specific stock I have benefited from. I will outline the best US stocks, the best Canadian stocks and the best "penny stocks" out there at this time...as well as tell you how to continue to research many dozens of other specific stocks for yourself and determine which stocks are worth your hard-earned bucks. But even if you don't want to do ANY research, the stocks outlined in this book will give you guidelines on which specific stock to buy NOW to cash in on the eminent bonanza.

NOTE: as of this writing (end of December, 2018) tariffs, trade wars and an unstable administration have led to a huge decline in stock prices across the board. As Warren Buffet said,

"Be fearful when others are greedy. Be greedy when others are fearful."

NOW is the time to buy!

NOTE: No one can guarantee anything in life, let alone stock prices. This book is meant to provide information for prospective investors and does not recommend purchase of any stock, guarantee profits or make any other promises specifically or implied.

Choosing A Broker

First of all, you want a broker that allows you internet trading options. You can place an order to buy or sell at any time 24/7 via the internet but the actual purchase or sale will only take place during the NY stock exchange hours which are 9:30 AM to 4 PM Eastern time, weekdays.

In the online arena, until recently there were four giants: TD Ameritrade, Scottrade, Options Xpress and my favorite, ETrade. However, Scottrade was recently subsumed by TD Ameritrade, so, now there are tree. Of the three, there are only two I would consider because Options Express has a $14.95 minimum quarterly fees and a very confusing (at least to me) fee structure. (many brokers now offer online trading, but I address here those exclusively online). That leaves the following two:

E*TRADE: (the one I use)

https://us.etrade.com

They have a $1,000 deposit minimum to open an account. Your "account" includes cash on hand you can invest at any time AND all stocks held at any given time. Each buy or sell is a flat $6.95. I particularly like E*TRADE because of the simplicity of online buy/sell functions AND because the provide FREE phone help 24/7 to "walk you through" any process and answer any question. The agents are always polite and well informed and more than willing to "educate" you on any questions or areas of interest you may have. No other fees other than the flat rate trade fee and they will even cover your bank's fee to wire $ into your account the first time. After that, they will help you set up a direct link to your bank account so you can request a transfer without your bank charging you a wire fee. Super easy-peezy.

In addition, they provide 1 day, 5 day, 3 moth, 1 yr, 3 yr and 5 yr graphs of the price fluctuations of each stock you have under consideration. NOTE: all graphs in this book are from E*TRADE.

DT Ameritrade:

www.tdameritrade.com/

While I have no personal experience with them, research indicates they provide a nearly identical service to E*TRADE, with the same $6.95 fee per trade BUT they have <u>no minimum</u> to open an account with them. IF all other services are the same, this may be the way you want to go, and absolutely the way you want to go if you have only $100 to $200 with which to start off. **NOTE:** Once you have a broker you can increase your account by simply filling in the transfer portion on your broker's site every payday, transferring in $25, $50 or more each payday. If you start off very small, this would allow you to get in while the getting in is still good.

Preferred   US   Companies

(Remember, we are, at this moment at a low stock market "crash" but the marijuana industry is inevitably going to explode, so, low prices now mean it is the ideal time to buy)

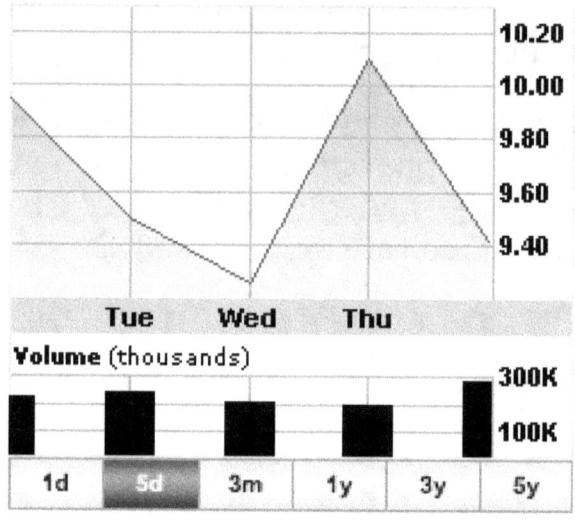

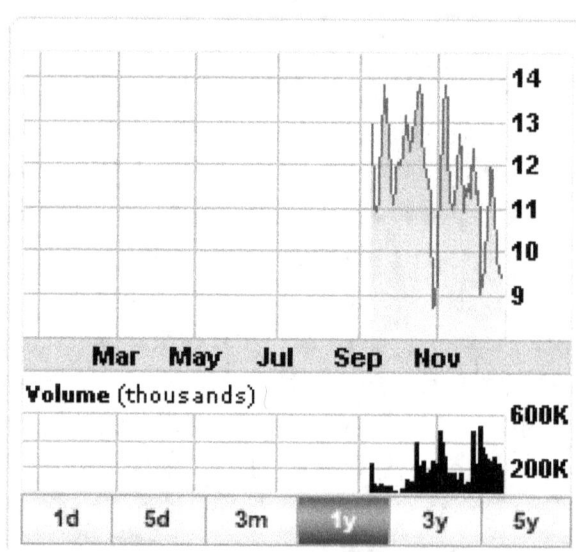

CHARLOTTES WEB HLDGS INC COM (CWBHF)

Price   12-22-2018: $9.419

This company is THE medical marijuana dream. The seven brothers who developed the strain, "Charlotte's Webb" did so at the request of parents of a young girl suffering hundreds of seizures daily and whom the AMA had given up on and told the parents to prepare for her death. This strain is THE IDEAL strain from which to isolate CBDs, the major component (and non-psychoactive) for medical use. Even better, used strait it provides even stronger benefit due to something called "the entourage effect." The strains considered to be "high in CBDs usually have 2 to 4% CBD content – Charlotte's web has 42 to 47% CBD content! This company is the market leader in the production and distribution of innovative hemp-based cannabidiol ("CBD") wellness products. This strain in by far the best strain from which to concoct CBD treatment and, therefore, is inevitable to succeed. Furthermore, the brothers never allow seed to flow out of the company. There is talk of MedMen buying the company, but that would only mean higher stock value. I consider this one of the few "sure thing" stocks available.

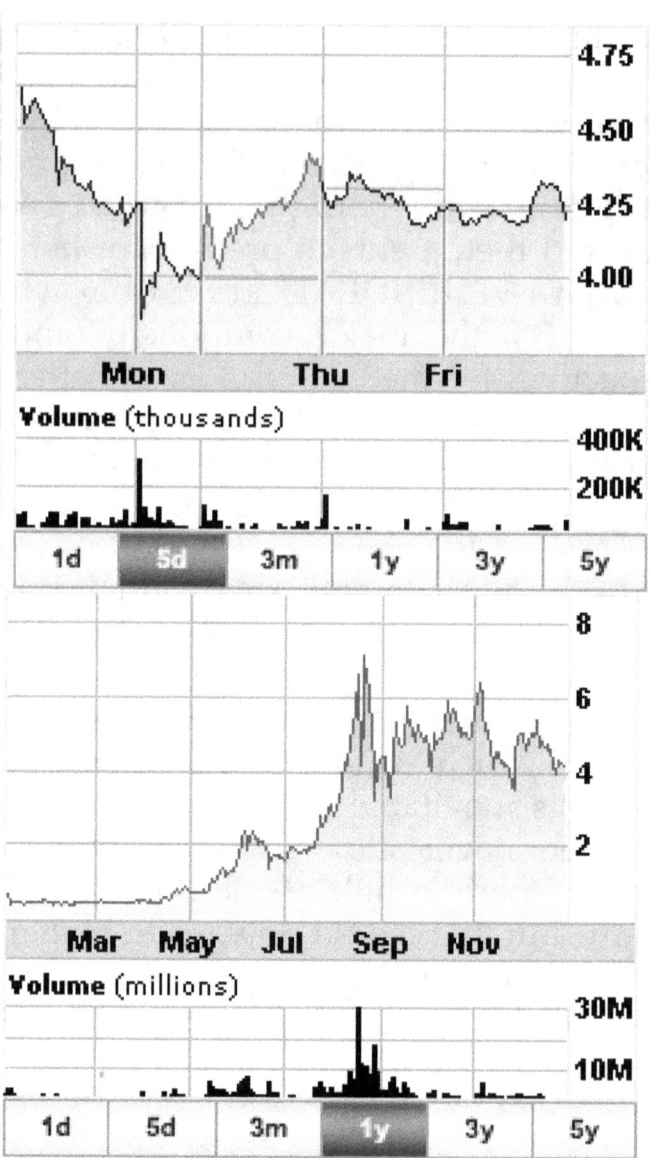

CV SCIENCES INC. COM (CVSI)
Price as of Dec. 30, 2018 $4.20

#1 leader of all marijuana stocks in 2018 up 554% in that year (1 day left)This corporation produces a number of cannabinol based products and is pursuing FDA approval for various products. In 2018 they experienced substantial revenue growth. They have a number of products awaiting clinical trials and look to be a very promising investment at this time.

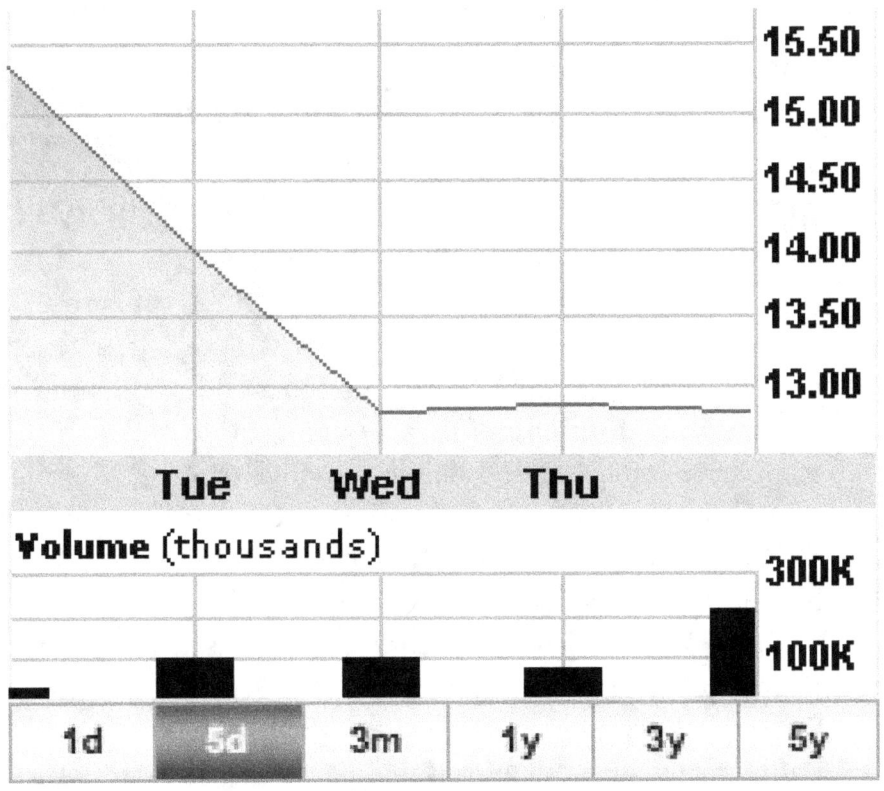

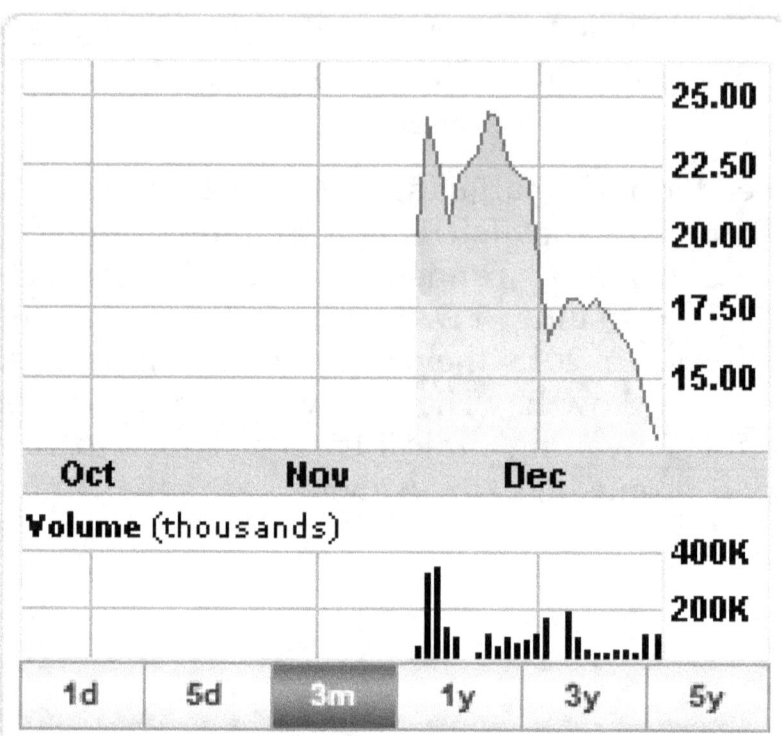

| 1d | 5d | 3m | 1y | 3y | 5y |

ACREAGE HOLDINGS INC COM SUB VTG (ACRGF)

Price Dec. 22, 2018: $12.79 Launching in 2014 it is run by former Wall Street banker Kevin Murphy. However, former Republican Speaker of the House John Boehner is -not the only former politician with a huge stake in the company; after taking over of High Street Capital Partners, Acreage appointed former Conservative Prime Minister of Canada Brian Mulroney to board seats. Other board members include former Massachusetts Gov. William Weld, former telecom CEO Larissa Herda and former IBM CFO Douglas Maine. Acreage Holdings is the largest cannabis company and in 18 states in the U.S, with over 40 dispensaries as well as cultivation operations in Oregon, California, Iowa, Illinois, Ohio, Pennsylvania, Florida, New York, New Jersey,

10

Maryland, Connecticut, Massachusetts, New Hampshire and Maine. Don't be deceived by the Dec. price dive. This company is poise to make a killing.

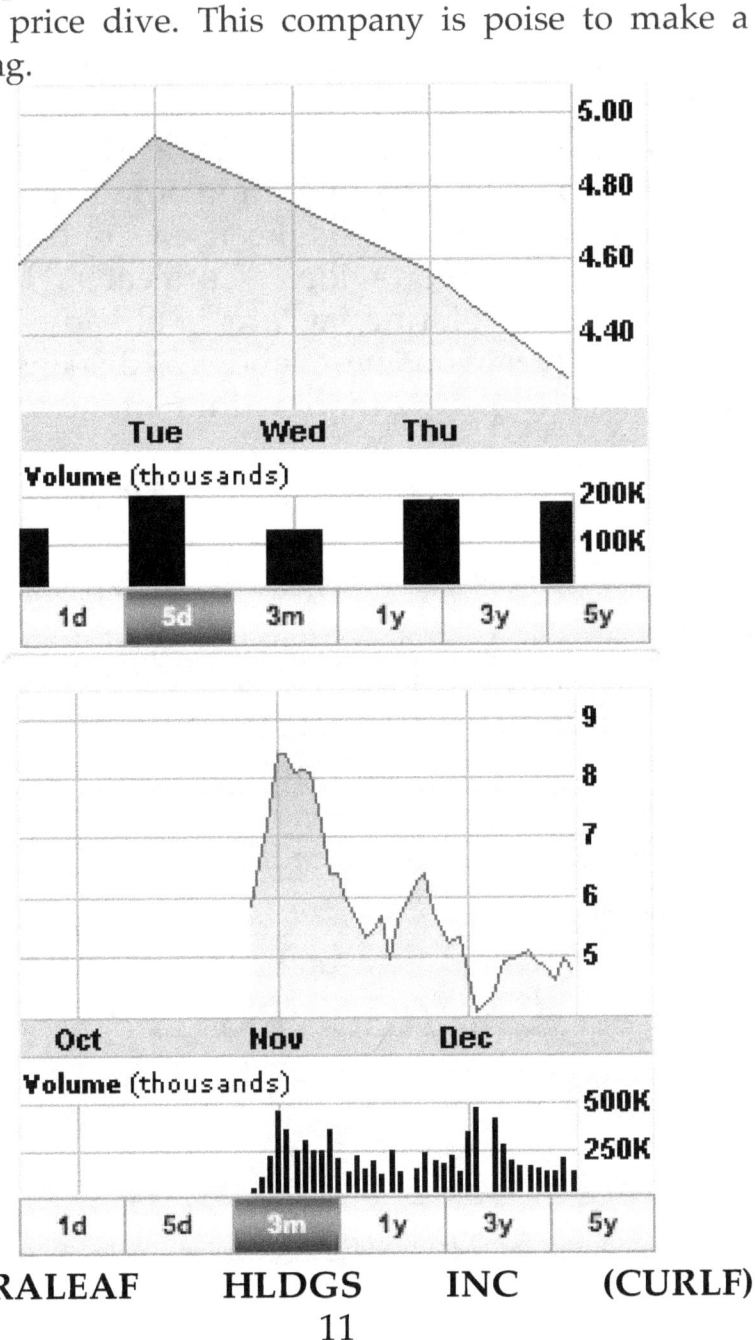

CURALEAF HLDGS INC (CURLF)

Price   **12-22-2018:**   **$4.276**

With CEO, Joseph Lusardi this company has had a $400 million equity raise and recent listing on the CSE. Curaleaf operates in the United States and sells 90 percent of what the company cultivates and produces in its own dispensaries. The company will be operating in 12 states by the end of 2018 and is licensed to open 69 dispensaries nation-wide. Curaleaf's largest presence is in Florida, where it already has a strong delivery business and 13 dispensaries, with plans to open 22 more within months.

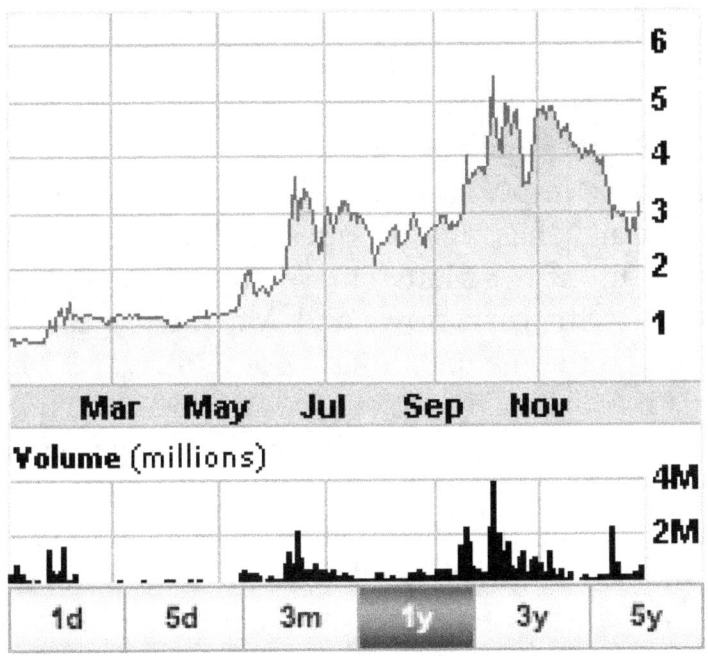

MARIMED INC COM (MRMD)
.Price 12-30-18: $3.125

#2 top performing marijuana stock of 2018. With growth of 353% in 2018 (one day left). Is a multi-faceted company which covers many aspects of the marijuana industry. Including marijuana production facilities in five different states and performs consulting services to other marijuana companies. Owning a number of subsidiaries, which produce marijuana products from cannabis strains to cannabis infused edible products, including Kalm-Corn popcorn and Betty Eddie's fruit chews. Its growth depends on continued expansion and is already looking to development in five more states

13

including New Jersey, Michigan and Florida. Michigan and Florida alone could represent more than $1 billion in annual revenue just in those states. Their financials have strengthened in 2018. Their most important financial dynamic is cash on hand, which has almost quadrupled in size in the past 6 months. Many marijuana stocks have a problem with cash flow, and MariMed's cash flow strengthen them substantially going forward. Market size is important in pot stocks. MariMed focuses on the US market and the US market is projected to reach $22 billion in the next 5 years (though, this could be a significant underestimation but certainly not an over estimation). That is at least 3 times the size of the Canadian market. While there is always risk with stocks, MariMed looks like a good one.

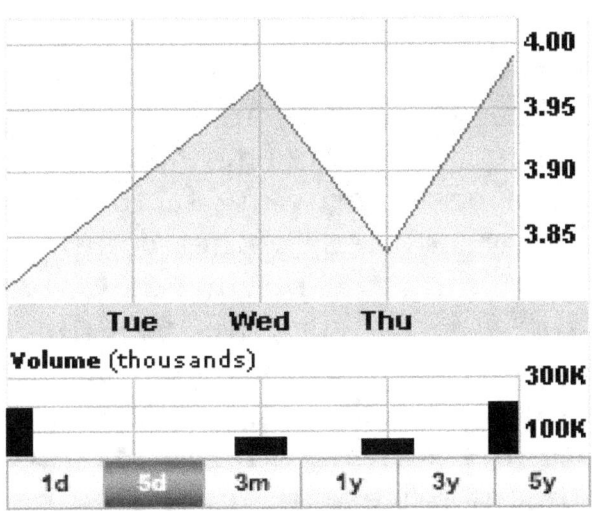

IANTHUS CAP HLDGS INC COM (ITHUF)
Price   12-30-18: $3.99
#4 earner 2018 up 70%. Avoids the bigger
markets like Colorado and California,
focusing on less competitive ones.
Headquartered in New York, it is one of
only 10 companies allowed a license to
cultivate marijuana plant in NY state. A near
40,000 square foot facility will provide year
round cultivation and will supply 2,400
kilograms (5,200Bs)per year to the domestic.
This is just to start – plans are to provide
over 125,000 square foot of growing space. A
subsidiary company, Mayflower Medicinals.
will build a 36,000 square foot growing
facility in Massachusetts. Their
GrowHealthy subsidiary is contracting
agreements for 15 dispensary facilities in
Florida. The Sunshine state is currently the

15

4th largest in terms of medical marijuana patients. The focus on medical marijuana rather than recreational. There are also plans for a Florida based growing facility as well. The firm also acquired 2 other companies in the past year after the buyout of Citiva and GrowHealthy. However, this is still a very small company, with total revenues of just $3.2 million reported for Q1 2018. However, MPX is joining Ianthis around January 19th, sotheir current price will be a bargain and a good opportunity for investors.

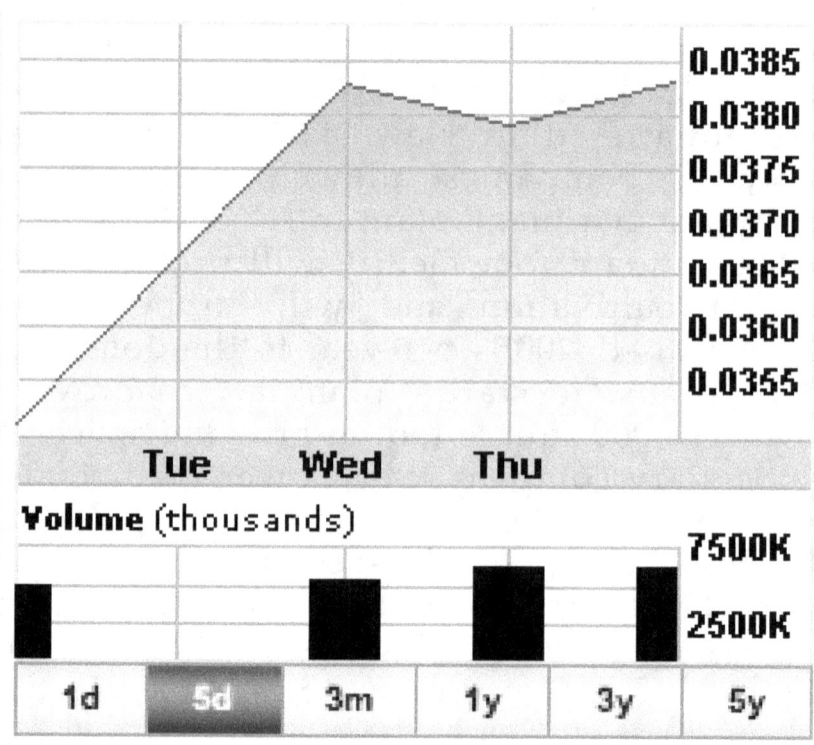

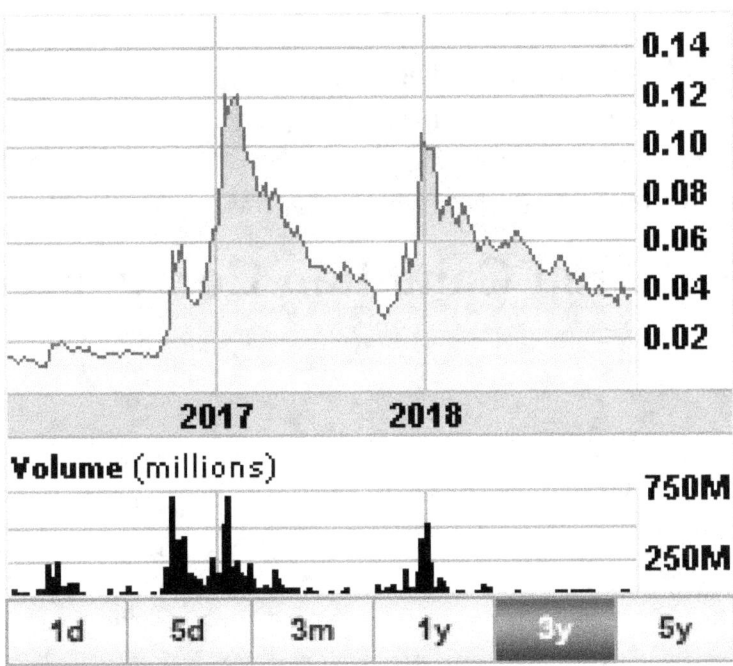

0.14
0.12
0.10
0.08
0.06
0.04
0.02

2017   2018

Volume (millions)

750M

250M

| 1d | 5d | 3m | 1y | 3y | 5y |

CANNABIS SCIENCE INC COM (CBIS)
Price   Dec.   29,   2018 $0.0383
NOTE: this is the exception to the rule re penny stocks. I am not afraid of having more than 5% of my portfolio in this particular penny stock. This is a US based company engaged in medical marijuana research and development. The Company works on phytocannabinoid science focusing on critical illnesses. It adheres to scientific methodologies to develop, produce and market phytocannabinoid-based pharmaceutical products. It is involved in the creation of cannabis-based medicines, both with and without psychoactive properties (THC), to treat disease and the symptoms of disease, as well as general health maintenance. It's focuses is on development of governmentally approved pharmaceuticals, including CS-TATI1, CS-

S/BCC-1 and neurological therapy under study or development. The Company's subsidiaries include Cannabis Science BV and Cannabis Science International Holding BV.

Preferred Canadian Companies

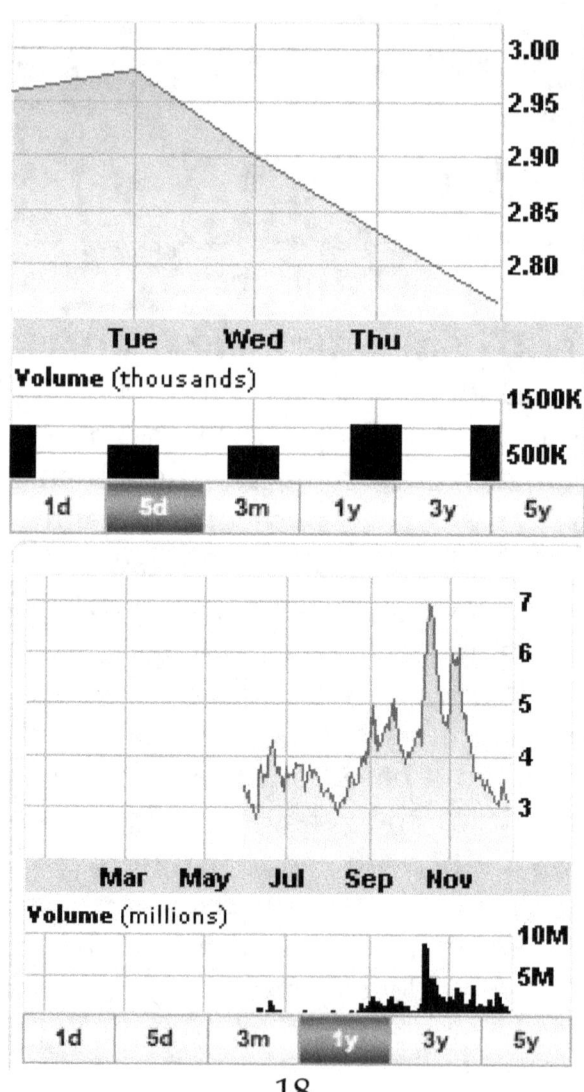

MEDMEN ENTERPRISES INC (MMNFF)
Price   12-22-18: $2.76
This is one company I am crazy for....and
with good reason: First, they are Canadian
based, so do not face the financial
restrictions of US companies, preventing
them from using banks, prevented from
having their stock purchased by Investment
Portfolios and unable to get bank loans due
to federal restrictions... but they have
spread over 12 US states, opening
dispensaries in THE priciest areas in major
cities. As a result, they are earning more
money per square foot than Apple (which
led at $3,000/sq.ft followed by Tiffanies, etc.
Medmen generate 6,500/sq.ft!) Also, there
is a rumor they might purchase Charlotte's
Webb, which would be a huge bump
for both company's stock holders.

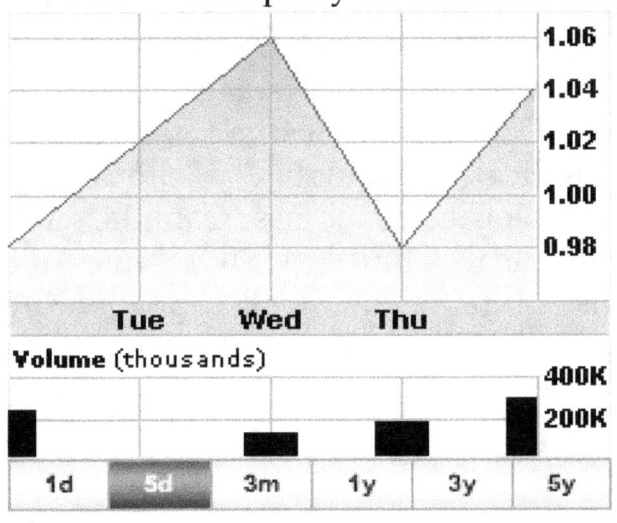

ALEAFIA HEALTH INC COM (ALEAF) Price as of Dec. 30.2018: $1.04 #3 in 2018 with a 90% increase in price. This company is Canada's largest network of referral-only medical cannabis clinics, with Twenty-two locations across Canada, Aleafia's Canabo Medical Clinics (CMC) have over 80 physicians utilizing medical cannabis therapy treating over 50,000 patients throughout Canada.

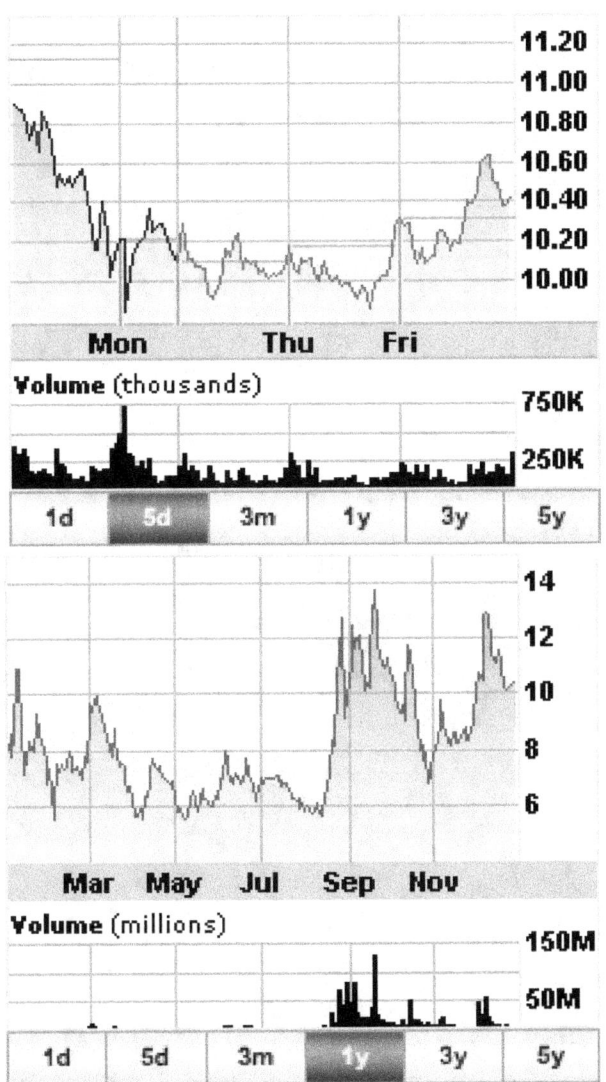

CRONOS GROUP INC COM (CRON)

Price Dec. 30,2018: $10.42

#5 highest earner in 2018 with a 29% price increase, this company is a Canadian grower and provider of cannabis for medical purposes and has world wide distribution. Given the daily price fluctuation of this stock you may want to place your buy bid accordingly to get it at a dip rather than place your bid at a peak.

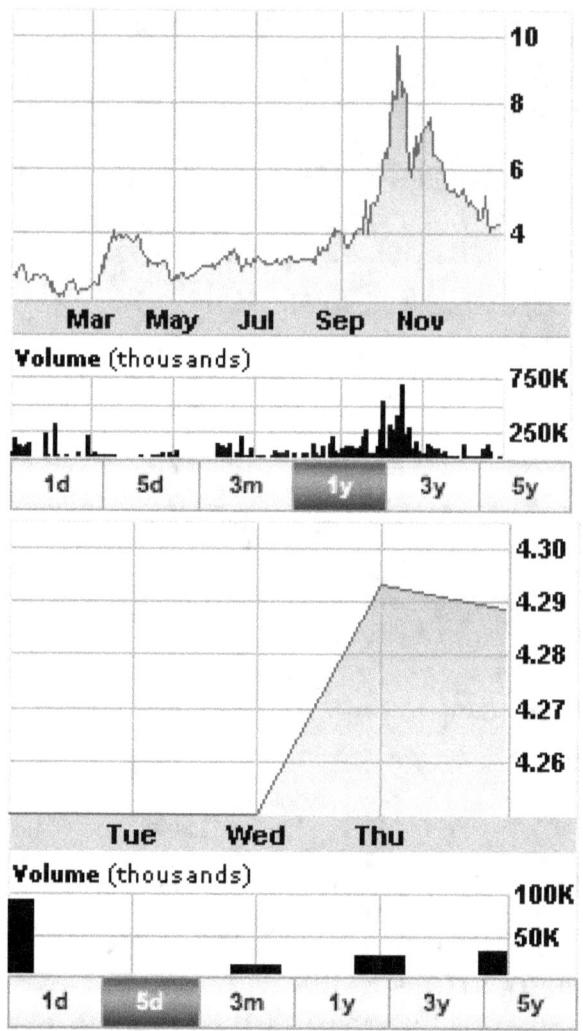

TERRASCEND CORP COM (TRSSF)
Price Dec. 30,2018: $4.289
#6 at a 26% increase but has seen its in 2018, this company was only formed in March 2017

market value surging to over $350 million in just a few months. The share price has continued to climb. It includes wholly-owned Solace Health, Terra Health Networks, and a 50% interest in Solace RX. The production is handled by Solace which operates a facility of 67,300 square feet in Mississauga. Solace received a cultivation license in June 2017 and secured its sale license in March 2018.

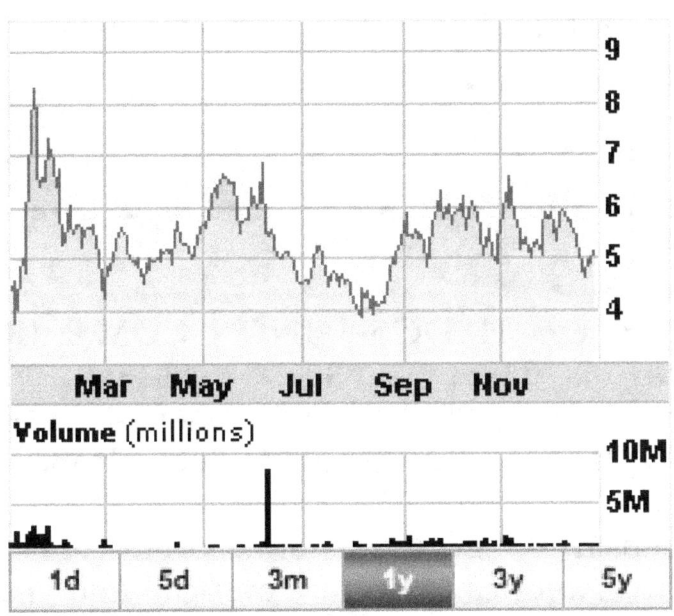

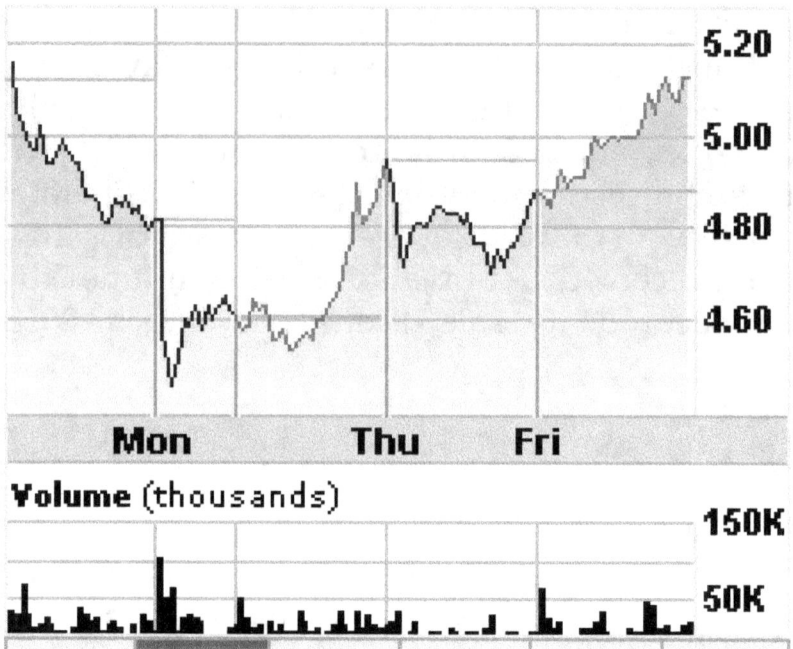

KUSHCO HLDGS INC COM (KSHB)
Price Dec. 30 2018: $5.13
#7 in 2018 at 25% increase, they service more than 5,000 legally operated medical and adult-use

dispensaries, growers, and producers across North America, South America, and Europe. While KushCo services all facets of the cannabis industry, it has no direct involvement with the cannabis plant or any products that contain THC or CBD themselves.

25

INNOVATIVE INDL PPTYS INC COM (IIPR) Price Dec. 30,2018 $45.89 making this company #8 for 2018 at a 22% increase for the year. Innovative Industrial Properties, Inc. is the first and only real estate company on the New York Stock Exchange (NYSE: IIPR) focused on the regulated U.S. cannabis industry. It acquired property in Barry, Illinois, which comprises approximately 75,000 square feet of industrial space situated on approximately ten acres. The purchase price for the property was $19 million. They also entered into a long-term, triple-net lease agreement with a wholly owned subsidiary of Ascend Wellness Holdings, LLC (Ascend), which intends to operate the property as a medical-use cannabis cultivation and processing facility in accordance with Illinois medical-use cannabis regulations. Ascend has raised nearly $40 million in capital to date, including from investors Poseidon Asset Management, Salveo Capital, JM10 Partners and Shire Capital Advisors, and has targeted Massachusetts, Illinois and Michigan as its initial states of operation.

CANNAROYALTY CORP COM (ORHOF)

Price   Dec.   30,2018: $4.87

#9 gainer in 2018 at 18% increase. CannaRoyalty is just now leveraging two prominent California-grown distributors to build the pre-eminent third party distributor in the state which will create a leading distribution business in California, the world's largest regulated cannabis market. Success in this enterprise combined with their recent $25 million dollar acquisition of 180 Smoke (which has 26 key dispensaries in Canada and is opening 10 new ones) could lead to Humongous gains.

CANOPY GROWTH CORP COM (CGC)
Price Dec. 30, 2018: $27.37
#10 at 6% increase in 2018, it is currently the world's largest medical cannabis company, operating 10 licensed cannabis production sites, four main street locations in Ontario, and has operations in 11 countries on five continents. Formerly Tweed Marijuana Inc). As a multi-brand company. CIt has multiple subsidiaries; Tweed Inc, Bedrocan Canada Inc, Tweed Farms Inc and Mettrum Health Corpand is engaged in the business of producing and selling legal marijuana in the Canadian medical market. It is also focusing on producing and selling marijuana in the recreational market in Canada. Its core brands are Tweed and Bedrocan. Tweed is a licensed producer of medical marijuana. Tweed's commercial license covers approximately 168,000 square feet of its Smiths Falls facility and allows Tweed to produce and sell approximately 3,540 kilograms of medical marijuana per year. Tweed's built-out production capacity is over 10 climate controlled indoor growing rooms. Bedrocan is a medical-grade cannabis. Bedrocan has an over 52,000 square feet production facility in Toronto, Ontario is licensed, and includes over 30 vegetative and growing rooms, and over three dispensing rooms. While other companies are focused strictly on the Canadian and US market there is still huge potential across Europe and Australia. In Australia Namaste has around 95% of the marijuana website traffic in the entire country. If Australia becoming legal in the next few years = huge boost for the company. So with all this good news, what's the downside for the

"Amazon of Marijuana?" Well, like any company in an emerging market, there are growing pains. The stock price fell 18% in Q2 2018 (before their earnings report) on the back of troubles with their NamasteMD web portal and mobile platform. This portal is vital for the company because it is what will be used in their prescription fulfilment websites, and thus a huge part of their business. As well as in the diagnosis of new patients (seriously, you will be able to book an appointment within the app on FaceTime and speak to a licensed doctor). Obviously, this is a massive hurdle for them to overcome going forward, and one people who are interested in this particular stock should monitor closely going forward. However, for an app that claims to be "as easy to use as UberEats", if they do get this right, then it could signal big things for the company and its share price going forward.

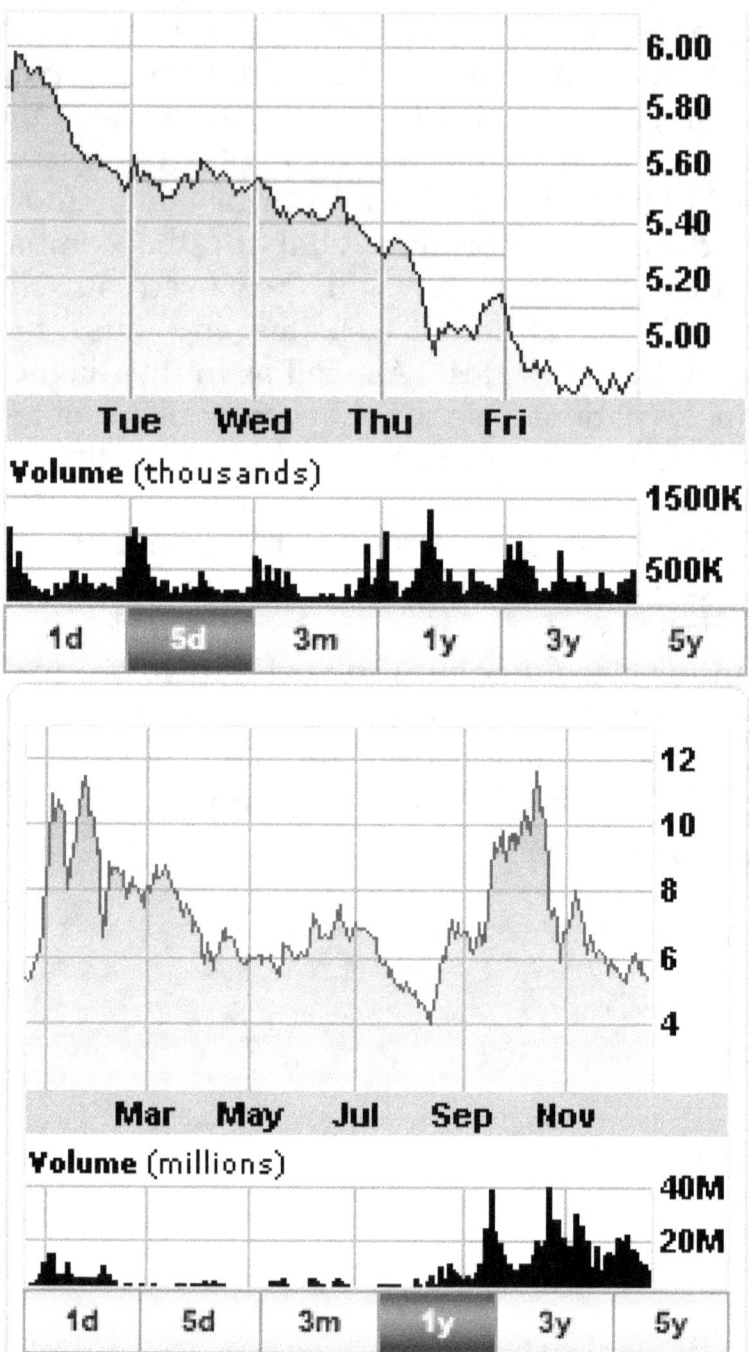

AURORA CANNABIS INC COM (ACB)

Price,   12-23-18: $4.88

Aurora is engaged in the production and distribution of medical cannabis. The Company is vertically integrated and horizontally diversified across every segment of the value chain including facility engineering and design to cannabis breeding and genetics research, cannabis, and hemp production, derivatives, home cultivation, wholesale and retail distribution. The Company's purpose-built facilities integrate technologies across all processes are defined by automation and customization. The Company has a funded capacity of more than 500,000 kilograms per year as well as sales and operations in more than 18 countries and on 3 continents, making them the 2nd largest cannabis company in the world. This is a rock solid company.

Penny Stocks Of Note

"Penny Stocks" are usually defined as any stock selling for less than $5, though the more commonly used definition is under $1 and sometimes as low as a fraction of once cent per share.

These stock are usually in companies operating on the edge, loosing money and looking for a breakthrough. They are considered "high risk" but potentially yielding very high rewards. These stocks should NOT comprise more than 5% of your portfolio. However, the potential upside is so great they should not be lacking from your portfolio altogether.

(Note: some very successful investors have HALF their portfolio in penny stocks! { but they pay close attention as to when to sell out at the top, as opposed to the long term investments mentioned in this book)

Namaste   Technologies   (NXTTF)
Price   12-22-18: $0.64

This company was dubbed the "Amazon of Cannabis" aiming to become an ecommerce giant in the marijuana market. Whether it can live up to its namesake is yet to be determined. However, they arelady are operating in over 20 different countries and on 30 different websites where they offer marijuana and marijuana related products including, but not limited to vaporizers, glassware and CBD products. They partner with producers and facilitates the sale of their products. Thier CEO, Sean Dollinger has founded and sold 4 successful ecommerce ventures before this. They already have achieved over 1.5 million worldwide users and sales ho9vering around $350 million. Revenue growth in 2018 was 32% and total revenues of $4.1 million. They were, in addition, just awarded a license by Health Canada, for the sale of medical marijuana online. They can now act as an online pharmacy, filling prescriptions for patients over the internet. This makes them the first website of its kind in Canada. They have. acquired the data and artificial intelligence software company Findify AB on late 2017. As a result, they are the marijuana company with the largest worldwide footprint.

Volume (thousands)

| 1d | 5d | 3m | 1y | 3y | 5y |

Volume (millions)

| 1d | 5d | 3m | 1y | 3y | 5y |

MPX BIOCEUTICAL CORP COM (MPXEF)
Price   12-22-18: $0.565
Bioceutical is attempting to put together on of the largest cannabis enterprises in the US. It has holdings in multiple states. It developed a high-margin wholesale concentrates business that has reached 40% of the market. In Arizona it provides staffing, procurement, advice, financial assistance, real estate rental, logistics and administrative services to three medical dispensaries in the "Health For Life" brand. also acquired "The Holistic Centre" dispensary this year. It also has two extraction and processing facilities in AZ. In Massachusetts it owns 51% of IMT, which owns a 40Ksq.ft. cultivation and production facility in Fall River and is licensed for three retail dispensaries through Cannatch Medicinals and construction has begun on the first dispensary. Since Mass. regulates the number of participants in the market, they have a distinct advantage. In California they have an extraction agreement with Case Farms Collective which has a 22Ksq.ft.facility for extraction and packaging in Long Beach and has agreed to distribute MPX-branded products throughout California, which has a huge market for both recreational and medical consumption. MPX also owns 99% of GreenMart in Nevada with a wholesale facility in Las Vegas which offers MPS extracts and edibles and is

capable of producing 85Kilos of concentrates per year. They also own 100% of the shares of Canada in Ontario, Canada which was licensed in 2017 for cultivation and has a 12,000 sq.ft. facility with a capacity of 1 to 2 thousand kilos. They are also developing a production facility over 72,000 sq. ft. in Owen Sound with a capacity for future expansion totaling 475K sq. ft. capable of annually processing over 8 thousand Kilos of flower and 317 Kg of concentrate. MPX also manages three dispensaries and one producer in Maryland. Many believe this is THE best penny stock available.

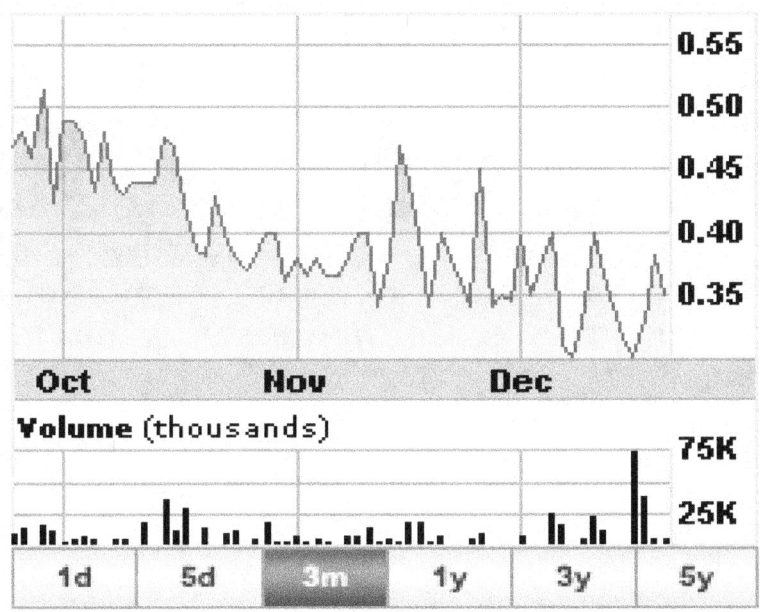

SUNSET IS GROUP INC COM NEW (SIGOP)

Price as of 12-22-18:$0.350 Currently down from 50c in Oct, but there are dynamics at play which indicate this company should not be dismissed yet. It received a growing and cultivation license in January and its location in California gives it a leg up to capitalize on the growing of recreational marijuana for the huge market in California. The company plans include expanding to over 750,000 square feet of growing space. Much of this expansion will be funded by equity agreements rather than by debt which so many other penny stocks rely on hoping for one big breakthrough. They have also promised no share dilution either. It also has a diversified product line including pre-rolled marijuana cigarettes in addition to the dry flowers it grows and them sells to dispensaries. Overall this California grower, is worthy of consideration due to their ambitious management team and aggressive plans for expansion.

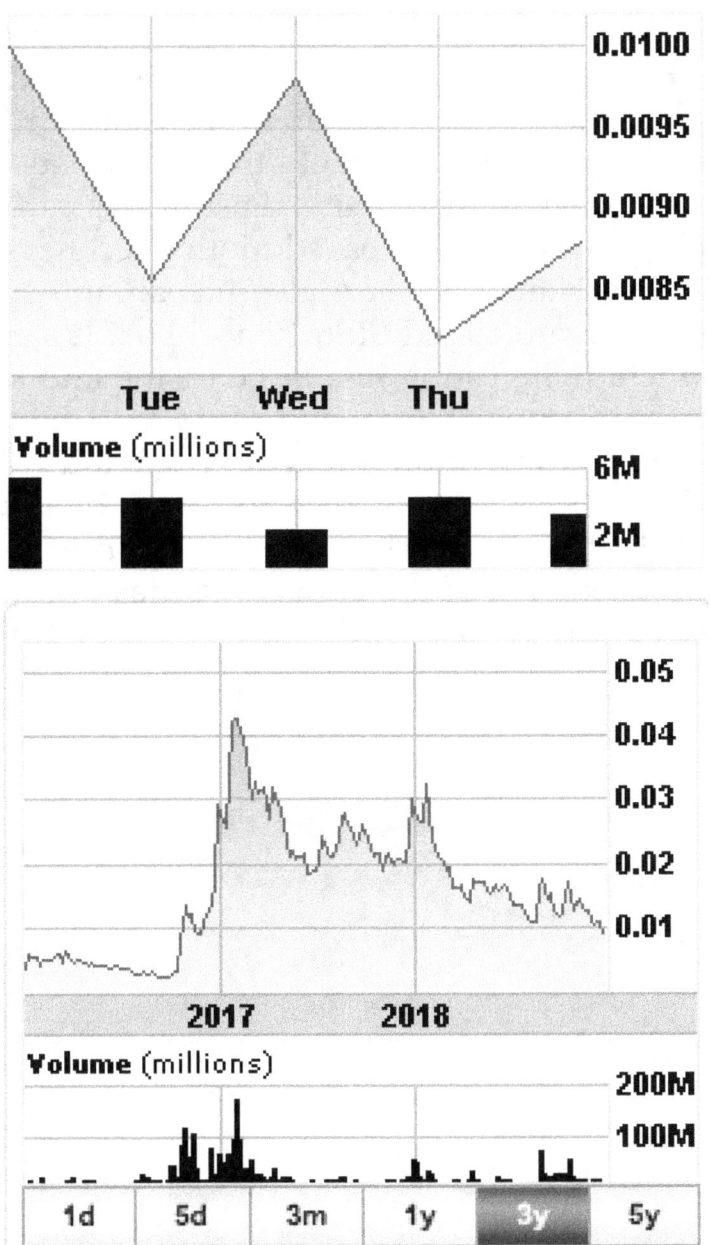

EASTON PHARMACEUTICALS INC COM (EAPH)   Price   Dec.   22,2018:   # 0.0088
A pharmaceutical company focused on the general consumer market than any specific disease prevention or cure. Easton has already developed a Cannabis based motion sickness get known as Nauseogel and also has an anti-aging skincare cream called Skin Renou HA. It's goals also include investing in a large casino and hotel resort in Europe. This move could well pay big time, depending upon financing used and where that leaves the company. In addition, it does hold the potential to market marijuana directly to casino goers. All of the above qualifies this stock as   worthy   of   at   least   monitoring.

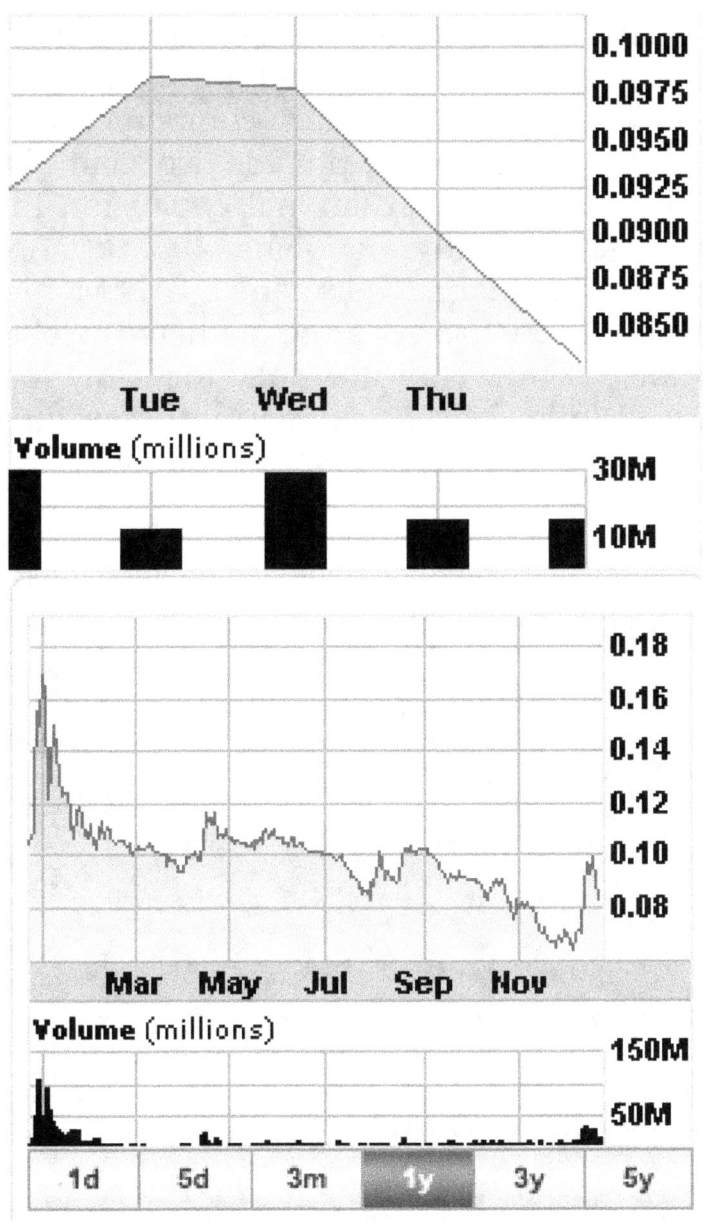

MEDICAL MARIJUANA INC COM (MJNA)
Price Dec. 22,2018: $0.0832
One of the more well known, MJNA was the

43

first publicly traded marijuana stock and producers a variety of CBD products. It also owns a number of subsidiary companies such as the HempMeds brand in Mexico and Brazil which makes for international expansion in the future. Additionally, it owns 40% of AXIM, another marijuana company. AXIM is a pharmaceutical firm dealing with the problems associated with clinical trials for CBD based drugs. While MJNA is currently profitable, AXIM is not. This stock is well liked by many.

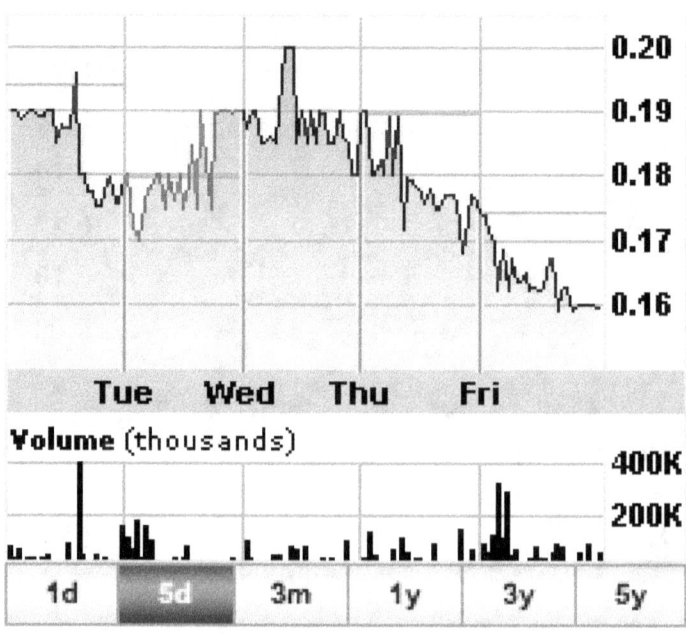

MCIG INC COM (MCIG)
Price as of Dec. 24,2018: $0.1594
A small company that is both a grower and greenhouse construction company with a consistent goal of diversification as part of a medium term risk mitigation strategy. Not just relying on increasing square footage but also pm expanding into areas like CBD production, cannabis technology and in medicinal development, leaving it less exposed to the risks of oversupply or getting priced out of the market by larger producers. Another interesting area of potential growth is its advertising network. This is a platform which will allow advertisers on the internet to target cannabis users. This approach holds great potential because larger advertising platforms such as Facebook and Google AdWords do not allow any kind of marijuana

related advertising to date. In this respect, eCIG provides marijuana companies the ability to get additional market penetration and to drive traffic to their websites.

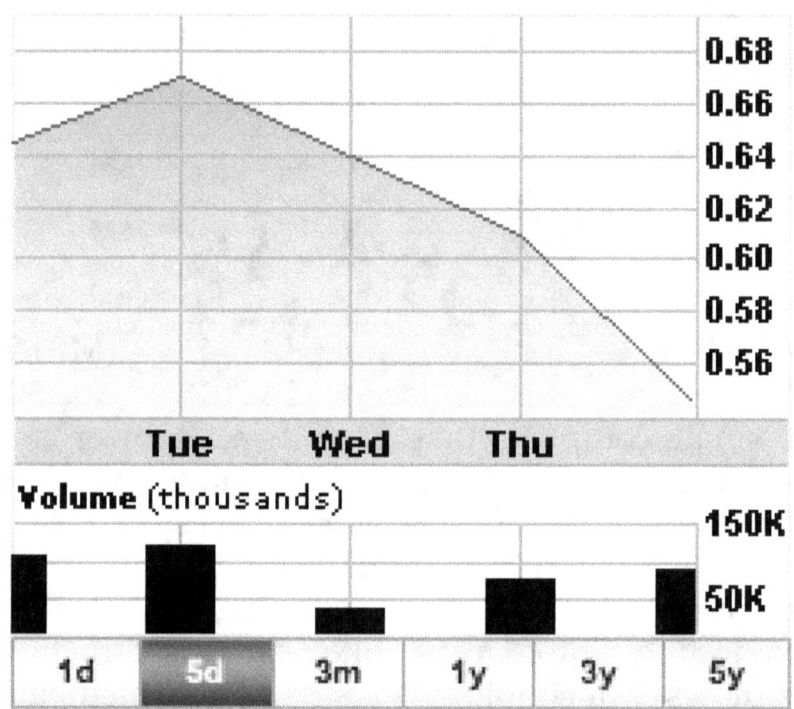

CANNEX CAP HLDGS INC COM (CNXXF)
Price: Dec.   22,2018: $0.546
The largest marijuana producer in Washington state and expanding into other states on the West Coast. An expansion into California is one that will continue to grow the company significantly. It acquired Jetty Extracts giving it entry into the growing vaporizer market as well. This is a huge move for its future as 50% of new marijuana customers are vaporizer users vs the ones who smoke dry flowers. As the market expands a lot more first time users come into the market, CANNEX will benefit directly. CEO Anthony Dutton has a firm vision for short to medium term growth, giving this penny stock a leg up on the others in its category.

47

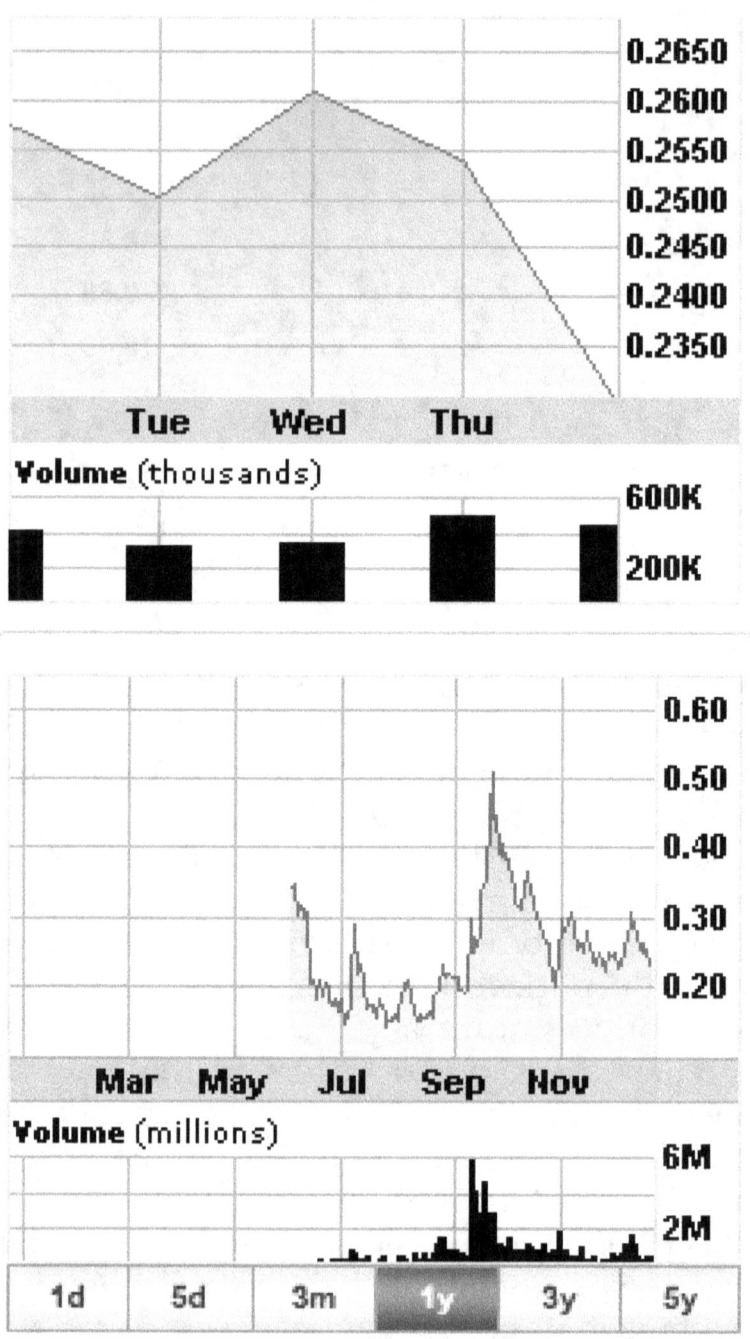

CROP INFRASTRUCTURE CORP COM (CRXPF)

Price as of Dec. 22,2018: $0.230
A multi-faceted marijuana company owning marijuana Canadian based properties, having a construction arm which builds large indoor growing operations and also provides agricultural equipment to new marijuana companies. They partner with new growers who have just had their license approved. This allows the growers to get a running start without having to invest large amounts of their own capital. In addition they just partnered with the Italian firm, XHemplar on a giant plantation with a 522,000 square foot facility which will be 30% owned by Crop Corp and will be the largest in Italy. Expected to yield around 20,000 Kilos of low THC, high CBD cannabis in the first year. Italy is a trailblazer when it comes to marijuana in the European market. It has been legal for medical use since 2006 and demand has outstripping supply until recently requiring much of the country's medical marijuana to be imported from the Netherlands and Canada. Consumptions levels have increased nearly 1,000 % over the last 4 years, and the nation shows no signs of slowing down. As Europe continues to awaken to the medicinal benefits of marijuana, partnerships like this will be invaluable in expansion outside of the high competition domestic market. Based the

Italian deal alone, it is reasonable to expect this now penny stock could move into the big leagues in the very near future.

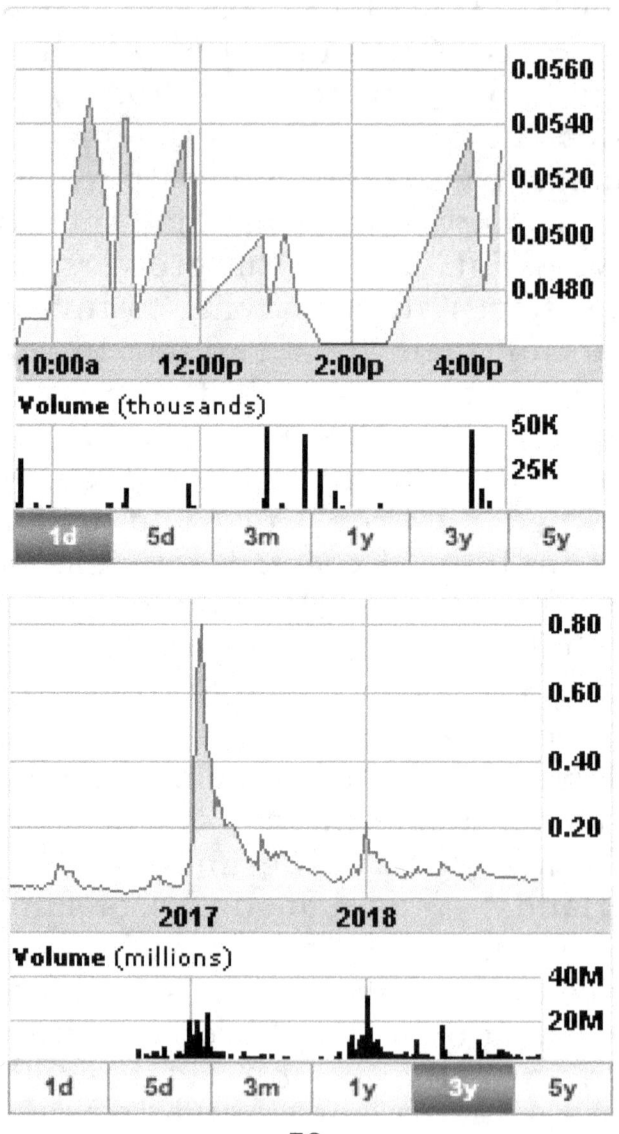

MOUNTAIN HIGH ACQUISITIONS COR
COM (MYHI) Price 12-22-18: $0.053

A holding company that helps provide cannabis providers with the funding to grow their business. One thing they launched is an initiative to help cannabis producers increase the yield per square footage while a lot of the other companies focus exclusively on having the largest square footage growth sites. This factor could be extremely beneficial over the next one to two years.

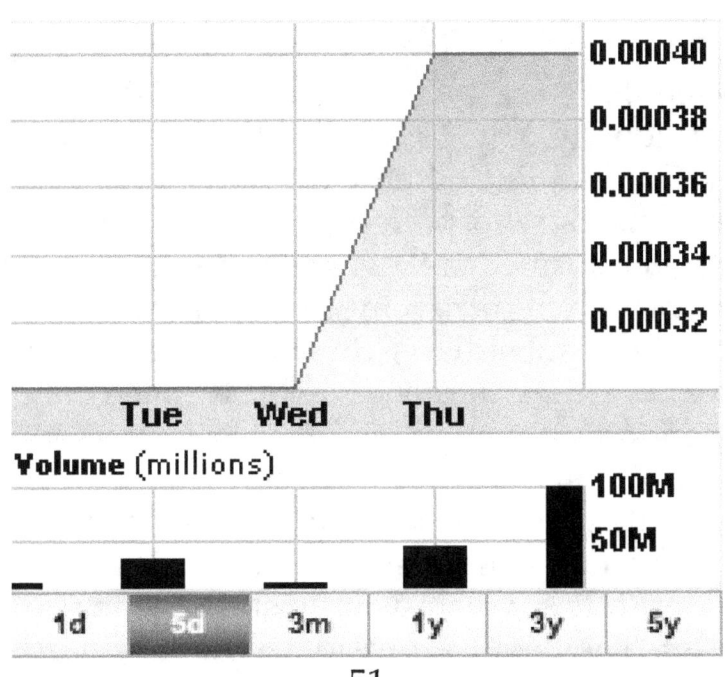

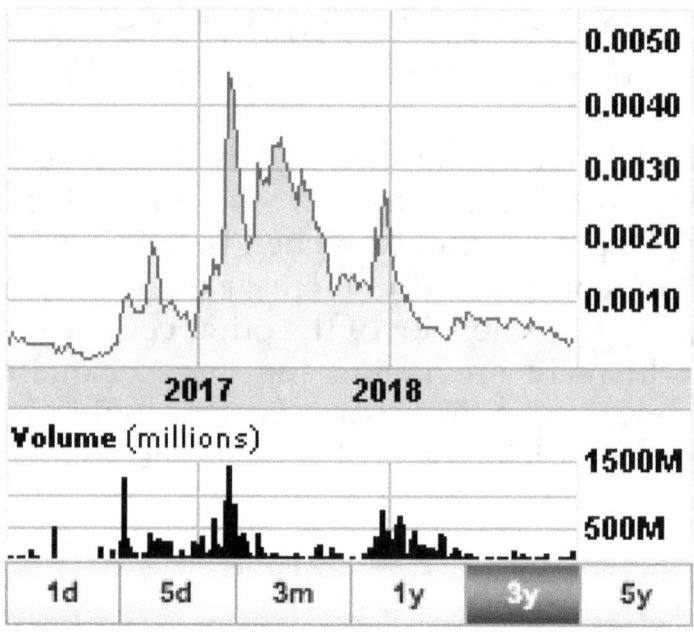

NEWGEN TECHNOLOGIES INC COM (NWGN) Price 12-22-18: $0.0004
Exceptionally low priced. Well known for their Easy Grinder line of herbal grinders - a favorite among users who prefer dry marijuana flowers. Last year formed an overseas distribution deal with the Dutch firm, Simply Green. Also recently formed the subsidiary, Royal CBD to go further into the CBD market, which is one that has tremendous potential. CBD is easier to sell and has no psychoactive effects, making huge contribution to the medical marijuana field and very popular with first time cannabis users and demographics which usually shun the marijuana market. They sold a subsidiary, Rich Cigars Inc. to pay off $2 million debt. Note: Newgen is also known as VaporGroup Inc.

Volume (millions)

| 1d | 5d | 3m | 1y | 3y | 5y |

0.0550
0.0525
0.0500
0.0475
0.0450

Tue   Wed   Thu

3M
1M

0.20
0.15
0.10
0.05

2017   2018

Volume (millions)

50M
25M

| 1d | 5d | 3m | 1y | 3y | 5y |

53

Player's   Network   (PNTV)
Price   12-22-18: $0.04862

Licensed in 2 separate states they primarily focus on the growing and selling of marijuana and also own WeedTV, an online social network channel for marijuana enthusiasts. This provides traffic to PNTV's holdings as well as producing ad revenue from other companies. They recently announced their best ever month of sales, which is an indication they are trending in the right direction. The company also recently acquired Green Leaf Farms Salinas Valley, which gives them more total square footage. Green Lead manufactures both dry flowers as well as other cannabis products like oils and extracts.

GOLDEN LEAF HOLDINGS LTD. (GLDF
Price 12-22-18: $0.080

This company's goal is to be the McDonald's of the marijuana industry. It's ultimate goal is a set of brand name franchises across the US, Canada and Europe. The stated goal is in having a trusted name, customers can rely on for consistent flowers and product quality around the world. They have a chance of winning over the local customers They announced a takeover of Nevada based Tahoe Hydroponics in August 2018 which shows their determination to scale quickly over the next two years. Tahoe already has brand name recognition. Tahoe gives them exposure to markets in both Nevada and California and gives the Canadian firm a very strong presence in the US market. In addition, the two top Tahoe executives agreed to stay on for 18 months to oversee the transition. I like this company a lot. While it could go bust, if it makes it HUGE gains are possible with this one.

Companies Worth Further Research

While the earlier in-depth descriptions are companies I have looked into, there are over 650 now in the marijuana businesses. Below are lists available for further study as your portfolio expands:

The chart on the following page is from New Cannabis Ventures on December31, 218. However, you can always get the latest update online at:

https://www.newcannabisventures.com/cannab is-stock-index/

Symbol	Company	Last	Chg	%Chg	Open	High	Low	Share Volume	Total Value	52Wk High	Market Cap
CGC	Canopy Growth Corporation	27.27	3.56	2.09%	27.12	29.06	26.18	4,353,686	N/A	99.25	9,360,451,990
TLRY	Tilray Inc.	75.15	4.07	5.73%	72.71	77.27	70.58	1,493,280	N/A	300.00	7,301,938,102
ACB	Aurora Cannabis Inc.	5.23	3.13	2.55%	5.06	5.38	4.98	11,908,602	3,107	12.53	5,219,041,518
GWPH	GW Pharmaceuticals Plc	95.40	1.04	1.10%	94.40	96.48	92.86	458,780	N/A	179.65	2,911,796,190
CRON	Cronos Group Inc.	10.42	3.13	0.97%	10.40	12.67	13.04	4,141,687	N/A	15.30	1,862,058,847
APHA	Aphria Inc.	6.36	3.69	12.39%	6.33	6.37	5.96	22,313,532	3,140	19.67	1,563,511,829
HYYDF	HEXO Corp - Ordinary Shares	3.52	3.38	12.21%	3.20	3.54	3.13	457,132	N/A	7.17	897,642,850
MRMD	MariMed Inc	3.13	3.47	17.48%	2.90	3.26	2.77	521,416	N/A	5.80	851,246,541
TGODF	Green Organic Dutchman	1.85	3.22	13.50%	1.89	1.94	1.64	344,659	N/A	7.89	496,326,701
IIPR	Innovative Industrial Properties Inc.	45.89	1.47	3.21%	44.97	46.61	44.65	130,046	N/A	55.63	448,611,462
OGRMF	OrganiGram Holdings Inc	3.43	3.31	9.64%	3.15	3.56	3.08	542,682	N/A	6.69	444,438,245
KSHB	KushCo Holdings Inc - Ordinary Shares	5.13	3.25	5.12%	4.91	5.18	4.77	463,596	N/A	8.51	400,005,458
CVSI	CV Sciences Inc.	4.20	-3.03	-0.71%	4.17	4.38	4.08	988,715	N/A	9.23	397,258,215
CBWTF	Auxly Cannabis Group Inc. - Ordinary Shares	0.61	3.03	5.19%	0.58	3.63	0.57	1,253,530	N/A	2.73	356,787,813
XXII	22nd Century Group Inc.	2.65	3.22	8.16%	2.46	2.68	2.43	1,774,185	N/A	4.44	329,665,890
GTBIF	Green Thumb Industries Inc	7.55	-3.13	-1.64%	6.26	9.08	7.48	1,302,316	N/A	25.00	319,825,299
CRHCF	CannaRoyalty Corp	4.87	3.48	10.93%	4.58	4.87	4.32	187,521	N/A	8.40	298,008,487
FSDDF	FSD Pharma Inc - Ordinary Shares - Class B (Sub Voting)	0.21	3.03	0.43%	0.22	3.22	0.20	704,300	N/A	0.88	268,135,842
SPRWF	Supreme Cannabis Company Inc - Ordinary Shares	0.95	3.09	10.23%	0.97	3.96	0.87	479,576	N/A	2.79	215,295,551
EMHTF	Emerald Health Therapeutics	1.61	3.29	17.41%	1.76	1.98	1.64	968,149	N/A	7.77	212,683,856

Bibliography

Dee,, Mickey, *Make Money Online With Cannabis Stocks,* **2018, Frazier Publishing & Services, North Las Vegas, NV**

E*TRADE
https://us.etrade.com

Hatcher, Peter PFA, *International Marijuana: The No B.S. Guide to Investing in Weed Stocks Globally,* 2018 Peter Hatcher

Heitz, Tim, multiple conversations 2016 through 2018.

Koovappadii, Easwar CPA, *7 Ways to Get Rich With Marijuana Stocks,* 2018 Classicanddigital Publishing, LLC

New Cannabis Ventures
https://www.newcannabisventures.com/cannabis-stock-index/

Options Xpress, now Charles Schwab
https://www.optionsxpress.com/

Satoshi, Stephen, *Stock Investing for Beginners: Marijuana Stocks,* 2018 Stephen Satoshi

Snow, Ted D, CPF, MBA, *Investing Quick Start Guide.* ClideBank Media, 2018

Thompson, Edwin (ET), multiple conversations in 2018

Author's Note: The content of this book is intended for research only. I am not suggesting any specific purchases and my own convictions are based on my personal experience and reference my own purchases and acceptable risks for myself. Any and all stock purchases always involve a gambol – I personally feel pot stocks hold the possibility of huge rewards.

If you liked this book you may also be interested in my #1 Selling book *THE ULTIMATE MEDICAL MARIJUANA STRAIN REFERENCE AND GROWING GUIDE: for Pain and over 120 other conditions (cross referencing over 500 strains)* **at:** https://www.amazon.com/ULTIMATE-MEDICAL-MARIJUANA-REFERENCE-GROWINGebook/dp/B0753FV4Y5/ref=sr_1_1?s=digitaltext&ie=UTF8&qid=1503863964&sr=11&keywords=Ultimate+Medical+Marijuana+Strain

To see all my medical marijuana books, visit
http://www.medicalmjinformation.com

If you enjoyed this book, PLEASE do not keep it a secret!

<u>Please leave feedback for this book</u> on the sight where you bought it. It will only take you one minute and it would mean a whole lot to me –Thanks! Michael